MW00511961

Heroes for Young Readers

Written by Renee Taft Meloche
Illustrated by Bryan Pollard

Gladys Aylward
Corrie ten Boom
William Carey
Amy Carmichael
Jim Elliot
Jonathan Goforth
Betty Greene
Adoniram Judson
Eric Liddell
David Livingstone
George Müller
Nate Saint
Mary Slessor
Hudson Taylor
Cameron Townsend

…and more coming soon.

Heroes for Young Readers are based on the *Christian Heroes: Then & Now* biographies by Janet and Geoff Benge. Don't miss out on these exciting, true adventures for ages ten and up! See the back of this book for a full listing of the biographies loved by children, parents, and teachers.

For a free catalog of books and materials contact
YWAM Publishing, P.O. Box 55787, Seattle, WA 98155
1-800-922-2143, www.ywampublishing.com

HEROES FOR YOUNG READERS

ADONIRAM JUDSON

A Grand Purpose

Written by Renee Taft Meloche
Illustrated by Bryan Pollard

YWAM
PUBLISHING
P.O. BOX 55787   SEATTLE, WA 98155

Adoniram Judson: A Grand Purpose Text © 2004 by Renee Taft Meloche Illustrations © 2004 by Bryan Pollard
Published by YWAM Publishing, P.O. Box 55787, Seattle, WA 98155 ISBN 1-57658-240-X Printed in China. All rights reserved.

A boy named Adoniram Judson
    was so very smart
he went to navigation school
    to study maps and charts.

He wondered if he'd sail the seas
    just like his grandpa had,
or be the pastor of a church
    and make his father glad.

Within his Massachusetts home
    his father often stated
how much God loves and cares about
    the people He's created.

When Adoniram's sister, though,
    got so sick that she died,
young Adoniram asked how God
    could let this happen—why?

As seeds of doubt began to grow,
    he kept these thoughts well hidden:
to question God at home for any
    reason was forbidden.

When he attended college in
     Rhode Island—near his home—
he found his questions and his doubts
     increasingly had grown.

So by the year of eighteen four—
     and after two school years—
the Christian faith he once had had
     began to disappear.

For Jacob, his good college friend,
     repeatedly had said,
"God may exist but does not love—
     you've simply been misled.
He wound the world up like a clock,
     then sent it into space
without a care for any life
     He's fashioned in this place."

Soon Adoniram turned away
    from all his father taught.
*The Christian God of love is just
    a fairy tale*, he thought.

Now he and Jacob liked to talk
    about their future lives:
once they were out of school, for what
    successes might they strive?

As soon as Adoniram
    graduated he agreed
to open up a school and teach,
    to meet a growing need.

He wrote two books, on math and English,
    but he soon grew bored.
And so he quit to search for greatness,
    riches, and reward.

He headed to New York, but found
    that jobs were hard to get.
With money running low, he grew
    more anxious and upset.

He left the city on his horse,
    deciding to head west.
One night—discouraged, and in need
    of somewhere he could rest—
he found an inn with one room left—
    occupied but cheap.
At least he could lie down there and
    would finally get some sleep.

A sheet hung down the middle of
        the room so it would hide
a man who groaned in anguish, dying
        on the other side.

As Adoniram tossed and turned
        and tried to sleep—in vain—
he thought about the man whom he
        heard crying out in pain.

He then recalled his college days
        with Jacob and their plans
to someday be important and
        to live lives that were grand.

I'm sure that Jacob's doing great,
        he thought, and knew full well
that his own life was joyless and
        was like an empty shell.

The hours passed. The sounds of
        suffering abruptly ceased,
and Adoniram slept a bit
        but with no sense of peace.

When Adoniram woke and went
    to breakfast, he was told
the man had died; that he'd been smart
    and wasn't very old.

And when the innkeeper told him
    the name of who had died,
poor Adoniram gasped! *Oh no!*
    He sat there horrified.

The man was his friend Jacob!
    His college friend was gone—
a friend who'd felt no hope that after
    death we still live on.

For several hours Adoniram
    sat, too stunned to move.
And when he rode away, the clopping
    of his horse's hooves—
in rhythm—seemed to sound the words
    that pounded through his head,
as he continued traveling west:
    He's lost. He's gone. He's dead.

An hour passed, and then he turned
    around and headed back
to where his parents lived—in search
    of something his life lacked.

He went to Bible school, and with
        his bright and well-trained mind
asked many thought-out questions about
        God and all mankind.

He read the Bible, studying it
        for months until he knew
for certain that God loves us; that
        the Word of God is true.

He realized then life should be lived
        for God and others too,
and prayed for God to show him helpful
        things that he could do.

One day he read about a place
        called Burma, where the king
and people did not know the one
        God worth our worshiping.

He thought, *Could this be just the challenge
        that God has in store?*
To go would give him purpose, something
        he'd been waiting for.

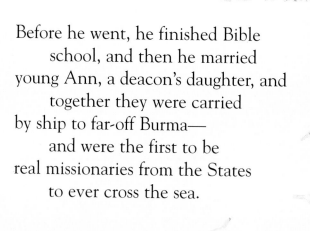

Before he went, he finished Bible
        school, and then he married
young Ann, a deacon's daughter, and
        together they were carried
by ship to far-off Burma—
        and were the first to be
real missionaries from the States
        to ever cross the sea.

They reached a town in Burma and
were greeted eagerly
by crowds of Burmese people full
of curiosity.

The older women dressed in long
bright tunics, and their hair
was pulled back in tight buns, and all
their children—brown and bare—
stood giggling as they poked at Ann's
strange western shoes, and then
a woman snatched Ann's bonnet off,
revealing her white skin.

The Judsons tried to learn the language
    spoken in that land,
so they could all communicate—
    listen, understand.

They learned the Burmese customs; most
    important was to know
to never use their feet to point
    or let the bottoms show.

And they must never stamp their feet—
    that simply was taboo—
and certainly the most insulting
    thing someone could do.

One day the city ruler's wife—
    who'd met and talked with Ann—
took her and Adoniram riding
    in a caravan
of elephants, which stopped in shade
    nearby a banyan tree.
They ate a scrumptious lunch and they
    were treated royally.

Now Adoniram wrote a book
    on what Christians believe.
This made the people glad, for they
    could read it in Burmese.

He bought an open building with
    a roof but without sides,
where Burmese people of all ages
    came from far and wide
to drink tea and ask questions about
    Christianity:
If Jesus was God's Son, why would
    He die so willingly?

To answer all their questions, he
    already had begun
to translate the New Testament
    into their native tongue.

One day the king of Burma died.
　　The new and reigning king
opposed all Christians everywhere.
　　All those caught worshiping
the Christian God were in great danger.
　　They could lose their lives.
The band of Burmese Christians wondered
　　whether they'd survive.

And yet they chose to take the risk.
    They secretly all met.
Unfortunately the degree
    of danger grew worse yet.

For while they took a chance to
    worship God, a war began:
a fleet of British warships came
    to try to take their land.

Soon Adoniram was arrested,
　　which was no surprise;
the Burmese king decided that
　　all foreigners were spies.

Since Adoniram's work on the
　　New Testament was done—
it had been nine long years of study
　　since he'd first begun—
he asked his wife to find a filthy
　　pillow and to hide
the only copy of the pages
　　of his work inside.

Ann brought it to his prison hut
　　and left it in his care.
Since no one else would touch it, he
　　could keep it safely there.

Months passed, until guards came for
　　Adoniram in the spring;
he clutched his pillow but was told
　　to leave the dirty thing.

He headed for the courtyard and
    then slowly turned around:
the guards had smashed his bamboo hut
    to pieces on the ground.

He saw his precious pillow in
    the middle of the pile—
his secret hiding place with work
    that had been so worthwhile.

He wondered as the guards locked him
    inside a cell-like place:
Has all the time I've spent translating
    been a total waste?

Then three months later Britain won
        the war and he was free
to go back to his home and live,
        but weakened physically
he prayed for strength to start on his
        translation work anew
so he could once again complete
        what took nine years to do.

A great surprise, though, lifted his
        low spirits from within.
A Burmese Christian came to visit
        with great news for him:
he said he'd gone to Adoniram's
        hut the very day
that it was smashed to pieces in
        the hope he'd come away
with some small token to remember
        him, but all he'd found
was Adoniram's dirty pillow
        on some muddy ground.

He'd brought it home and noticed all
    the lumps the pillow had.
When he'd investigated further
    he was very glad
to find the whole New Testament
    intact and clearly legible.
This find was more than luck—it was
    miraculous, incredible.

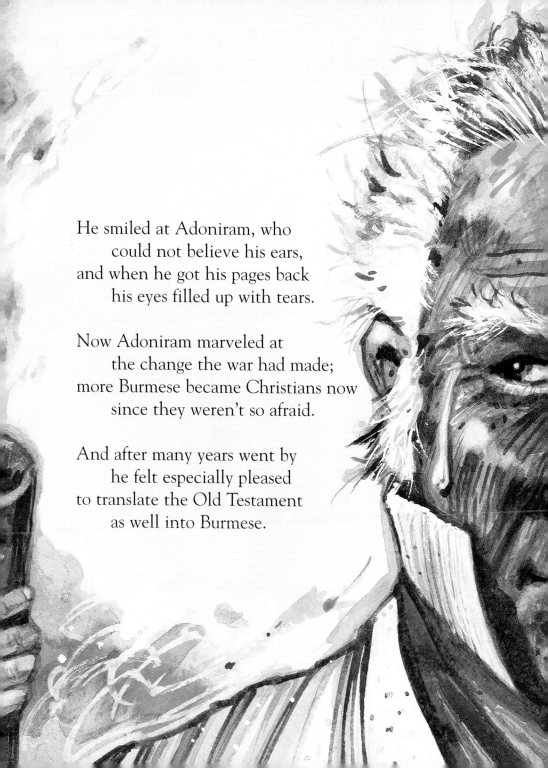

He smiled at Adoniram, who
    could not believe his ears,
and when he got his pages back
    his eyes filled up with tears.

Now Adoniram marveled at
    the change the war had made;
more Burmese became Christians now
    since they weren't so afraid.

And after many years went by
    he felt especially pleased
to translate the Old Testament
    as well into Burmese.

At sixty-one in eighteen fifty,
    Adoniram died.
But all the work he finished is
    still very much alive:
it's in the hands of people reading
    Bibles every day,
which tell about the love of God
    and show us all the way.

When we work out of love for God,
    at home or where we're sent,
the work we do with hands and hearts
    becomes our testament.

Christian Heroes: Then & Now
by Janet and Geoff Benge

Gladys Aylward: The Adventure of a Lifetime
Rowland Bingham: Into Africa's Interior
Corrie ten Boom: Keeper of the Angels' Den
William Booth: Soup, Soap, and Salvation
William Carey: Obliged to Go
Amy Carmichael: Rescuer of Precious Gems
Loren Cunningham: Into All the World
Jim Elliot: One Great Purpose
Jonathan Goforth: An Open Door in China
Betty Greene: Wings to Serve
Wilfred Grenfell: Fisher of Men
Adoniram Judson: Bound for Burma
Eric Liddell: Something Greater Than Gold
David Livingstone: Africa's Trailblazer
Lottie Moon: Giving Her All for China
George Müller: The Guardian of Bristol's Orphans
Nate Saint: On a Wing and a Prayer
Ida Scudder: Healing Bodies, Touching Hearts
Mary Slessor: Forward into Calabar
Hudson Taylor: Deep in the Heart of China
Cameron Townsend: Good News in Every Language
Lillian Trasher: The Greatest Wonder in Egypt
John Williams: Messenger of Peace

Heroes of History
by Janet and Geoff Benge

John Adams: Independence Forever
Clara Barton: Courage under Fire
Daniel Boone: Frontiersman
George Washington Carver: From Slave to Scientist
Meriwether Lewis: Off the Edge of the Map
Abraham Lincoln: A New Birth of Freedom
William Penn: Liberty and Justice for All
Theodore Roosevelt: An American Original
Harriet Tubman: Freedombound
George Washington: True Patriot

...and more coming soon. Unit study curriculum guides are also available.

For a free catalog of books and materials contact
YWAM Publishing, P.O. Box 55787, Seattle, WA 98155
1-800-922-2143, www.ywampublishing.com